THE $3000 BLUEPRINT

Income Acceleration Tactics for Launching Digital Products That Sell Themselves

GODWINS INKLINE

Dedication

Dedicated to Michael Inkline.

Copyright

No part of this book is allowed to be reproduced in any form without approval from the author.

Table of Content

CHAPTER ONE

Introduction

Making an extra $3,000 per month probably sounds like a pipe dream if you're stuck in a tedious 9 to 5 job that barely pays the bills. But what if I told you that you really can start earning a healthy side income online — maybe even replace your day job eventually — without a ton of experience or investments up front?

I get it. The idea probably brings up skepticism or downright disbelief. When I first heard people claiming to make thousands per month from their laptops, I rolled my eyes too. But after months of research, self-education and honing my approach, affiliate marketing, freelancing services and creating my own digital products allowed me to kiss my lousy corporate career goodbye. I waking up stress-free and living life on my own terms.

And I firmly believe anyone willing to put in the time and effort can accomplish similar results and start hitting that $3,000 per month goal. Sure, getting there may take patience, dedication to your craft and an acceptance that road bumps will arise. But armed with the proven online money-generating methods outlined in this book, you have an incredibly clear path to earning significant income each month. Income that provides true freedom: financial freedom, time freedom, career freedom, and freedom from worrying how to provide for yourself or your family.

So how do people exactly create this flexible online career and income really work? That answer unpacks into several pieces.

First, you need the right strategic frameworks and mental shifts regarding how to turn skills, knowledge or access to an audience into money online. The most successful people adopt certain core mindsets that optimize their chances for earning, ideating and persistence. We'll unpack key online money mental models so you can begin looking at income creation opportunities in an entirely new light.

Second, some basic tools and accounts lay the infrastructure for monetizing online.

For example, an email list manager, marketing analytics software, social media profiles, hosting for websites/courses etc. We will cover step-by-step how to set up the essential income generation tools with as little money spent up front as possible.

Third, we dive deep into several methodologies for actually making money online once your frameworks and tools are primed for monetization. Those primary methodologies include:

Affiliate Marketing: This powerful online income stream allows you to earn commissions by promoting other company's products and services. We will explore popular affiliate programs, tactics for driving targeted website traffic and common pitfalls to avoid. Even with little to no audience already, affiliate provides instant possibilities to monetize your online skills and start earning.

Freelancing Services: Online freelance platforms like Upwork, Fiverr and Freelancer contain endless money-making opportunities across areas like writing, graphic design development, virtual assistance etc. We discuss crafting compelling profiles, bidding for jobs, providing 5-star service to clients and other best practices to get your freelance income rolling in.

Creating Information Products: From online courses to ebooks, podcasts and beyond, information products leverage your expertise and allow profits from passive income streams. Make the product once and continue collecting income over months and years. We provide the blueprint for identifying profitable niche topics and getting your first digital product up for sale quickly.

This book elaborates on specifics so you can leverage any combination of those big three online money-making vehicles. Plenty of people consistently generate $3000+ per month with just one. But mixing income streams provides even more earning upside and diversification against issues affecting one specific source.

By implementing proven frameworks, monetization tools and income stream vehicles outlined, hitting a $3,000 per month goal becomes an obtainable feat, not some unrealistic pipedream. And reaching that benchmark means big things: quitting that miserable job, enjoying more flexibility and independence in your life on top building significant wealth over the long-haul.

True online income success does require consistent effort and embracing inevitable failures and roadblocks as learning opportunities though. Passive income rarely remains passive indefinitely without attention and refinement. You must constantly learn, adapt your approach based on results and apply targeted improvements.

But with deliberate, focused commitment to building these skills and online money vehicles this year, why can't it be you earning $3,000 next month? 10 years from now you may even laugh about when a measly few grand per month once seemed out of reach financially. When you put your future self in flexible, prosperous economic position the compounded personal benefits over time feel limitless.

Others are already doing it and now you can too by absorbing and applying the online income lessons and strategies across this book. Not overnight, but with dedicated effort you absolutely can hit impressive earning milestones month after month.

So buckle up, brew a fresh cup of coffee (maybe soon to be upgraded to your favorite glass of wine or fancy latte) and let's get you started on making some serious extra money online. The freedom and peace of mind you've been seeking awaits...

Why Make Money Online? Benefits & Motivation

If you currently slog away at a conventional job from 9 to 5, making an active side income online likely sounds appealing. And why wouldn't it be? Money making opportunities you can operate remotely provide game-changing lifestyle design, financial upside and personal growth potential compared to office grind.

But motivations behind earning online expand even wider when you dive deeper. Yes, dreams of exotic vacations and enjoying extra splurges motivate people to some degree. However, leveraging online income opens doors for incredibly meaningful quality of life upgrades beyond simple material wants.

For example, profitable online businesses and revenue streams allow:

Greater Location Independence

Want to spend winter months near sunny beaches with laptop in hand? Or visit family for a month without begging for time off from the boss? Location flexible online income lets you travel freely without restraint. Suddenly "working remotely" no longer caps out at a cramped home office space if money flows in from everywhere.

More Time & Schedule Freedom

Between tedious commutes and forced adherence to rigid schedules, traditional jobs usurp massive chunks of finite time. Hour long commutes alone account for entire unused weeks over a typical career. But by making money online, you seize control to focus efforts when feeling bright, inspired and energetic. Customizing schedules around personal or family needs becomes realistic when the office no longer dictates rigid routine.

Financial Security & Control

Rather than solely rely on a single job's mediocre paycheck under someone else's whims, online income diversity adds financial padding and autonomy. If one income stream stumbles, others keep personal economy intact and reduce risk. The comfort knowing you steer financial steering wheel outweighs depending on any boss for next month's rent money.

Career & Purpose Realignment

Let's face it – the vast majority of workers feel apathetic or downright disillusioned regarding conventional career paths. Online money opportunities open avenues to take professional skills into individually meaningful directions though, not just chase biggest paycheck out of necessity. Align work with passions by creating businesses around personal interests and values rather than merely tolerating paycheck drudgery.

Lifelong Learning & Growth

Continually learning, problem solving and mastering ever-evolving online skills keeps minds sharp. And unlike robotic office tasks, online income requires constant self-education to keep income flowing. Remaining a lifelong learner simply becomes part of the job description – a welcome feature for knowledge craving brains.

How's that for motivation?

The reasons above probably resonate as exactly why making consistent online income holds so much appeal and promise. At core, location freedom, financial control, time autonomy, reduced risk, passion pursuit and constant learning all equate to one supremely appealing end benefit: More ownership over your one precious lifetime.

Rather than allowing limitations of geography, office bureaucracy and someone else's schedule to rule life paths, online income vehicles hand individuals ultimate pilot control. Combined with pursuing meaningful work aligned with inner motivations and values, suddenly days transform into something far beyond monotonous means to a paycheck. Each moment opens up into an opportunity create, produce, explore and grow on your own often entrepreneurial terms.

Indeed, plenty choose online money goals simply to afford material wants like mansions or sports cars. Nothing inherently wrong with that. But recognize how the most fulfilled online earners chase far deeper life rewards than stuff. Their driving motivations come from seized control over how they spend their 24 hours, alignment with inner purpose and building lasting wealth even beyond what money can buy – growth, progress and making a difference.

So by all means set initial monetary benchmarks that ignite action or seem like pipe dreams right now. Let visions of future holidays, gadgets or donated piles of cash to causes you care about spark urgency today. But also know that freedom, purpose and fulfillment form life's most valuable currencies long-term. If nurtured properly, your online money journey plants seeds to cultivate profound life rewards money alone cannot buy.

Those deepest emotional, intellectual and purpose-driven motivations will fuel progress on days when financial goals alone wane as enough incentive. After all, anyone can earn another dollar. But redeeming more purpose-packed hours and realized human potential thanks to control over your schedule? That holds value beyond any dollar figure.

The diverse range of benefits making money online provides makes clear why this path toward income holds so much disruptive and lucrative potential for those willing to put in the effort compared to status quo career paths. When planned and integrated thoughtfully, online money vehicles allow people to architect lives of greater freedom and meaning.

Setting Realistic Income Expectations

When striving to make money online, one of the most important things is developing realistic expectations around how much money you can make and in what timeframe. Mastering patience and realizing quick, drastic income potential rarely unfolds overnight sets proper mindset for sustainable online income success.

So before diving in, reflect carefully on income objectives and adjust anticipated timelines if needed to align with common earning trajectory reality. That may require revamping beliefs if buying into get-rich-quick guru hype promising unfathomable sums after few weeks. While possible in rare cases, realize that statistical outliers and high failure rates among online income seekers signals standard paths look much different.

This chapter explores realistic monthly and yearly income ranges across three phases nearly all online earners navigate when building their profits over time. Bear in mind these phases often overlap and non-linear jumps occur too. But in aggregate, they represent general patterns for typical earners based on level of experience and scope of operation.

Phase 1: $0 - $500 Per Month

When initially exploring online income methods through vehicles like affiliate marketing, freelancing, social media monetization etc., view the first 6-12 months as an educational period testing what works without expecting to immediately replace full-time income. Consider any earnings during this phase as covering some life expenses or funding reinvestment into your online infrastructure versus solely paying the bills.

Focus priority instead on skill development across sales funnels, traffic generation, content creation and community building required for later profitability. This includes benchmarking effective marketing tactics, analytics tracking, operations infrastructure, and refining offerings. Assume at least 6 months ramp up time until income gains noticeable momentum.

Phase 2: $500 - $3,000 Per Month

As skills improve and visibility increases from an audience or marketplace, earning potential typically grows into modest part-time income levels, even bordering lower-tier full time income. For example, successfully securing recurring affiliate promotions, scaling a freelance service niche or attracting engaged social media followings enable monthly revenue scaling into this more intermediate bracket.

At this phase, online income earns the credibility and viability to justify dedicating more hours, assuming profitability merits allocating that time investment. Use portions of income generated to fund better infrastructure, digital advertising or product inventory once assured positive ROI. Avoid risky overeager splurging until income stabilizes though.

Phase 3: $3,000+ Per Month

After a year or more actively sharpening skills, the most resilient online earners gradually see incomes creeping toward sums allowing full financial self-sufficiency and livable solopreneur work. This income phase brings freedom to commit fully towards operating online businesses or monetizing personal brands given now sizable earnings.

Note that even at this level, income rarely scales overnight. Someone earning $5,000 per month online likely took years gradually building towards that amount through affiliate sales, info product launches, expanding a freelance team. etc. So continuing to reinvest portions of income into growth sustains momentum.

Again, these earning phase ranges depict broad expected trajectories, not rigid universally applicable sums. Plenty of outliers jump straight past Phase 1 with viral online content or leveraged skill assets gaining instant traction. And on flipside, Phase 3 sums might seem inadequate for supporting costs of living in high expense cities long-term. So adjust accordingly based on your unique situation.

Additionally, note most online earners generate income from multiple streams rather than a single source due to benefits like risk mitigation. So view income sums above as mixed contribution from affiliate earnings, digital product sales, creative services etc. Combining online income vehicles typically unlocks greater upside through complementing elements but requires initially ramping each one.

General Trajectory Takeaway

Making $10,000+ per month within six months online without existing audience rarely reflects realistic outcomes for most. Amassing immense income through sheer online marketing genius overnight proves more exception than rule.

But for those committed to iteratively mastering online money skills, building audiences and solving problems, noticeable income progress generally trends upwards over months and years. So rather than get rich quick, embrace a get rich slow mentality backed by a vision to earn, serve and provide long-term value. With consistent strategic efforts, earning potential typically ascends across the monthly income phases over time.

Again, outliers exist in both directions. Some enter online entrepreneurship with unique advantages like existing platforms or in-demand skills that garner quick income momentum immediately. Others struggle for longer duration before seeing meaningful profits. So adjust journey and expectations based on your distinct strengths and challenges.

Ultimately, dedicating consistent efforts towards serving people and progress compounds over the years to enable hitting impressive income goals. But obsessing over rapidity often distracts from effective skill building. Savvy online earners willing to patiently hone abilities and knowledge required in marketplaces often find themselves pleasantly surprised at how sizable that foundational base develops earnings over time.

So rather than enter online income seeking with get rich quick delusions, embrace reality that sustainable revenue requires slow and stable long game mentality. Building assets and enterprise value that pays compounding dividends over time trumps sporadic viral hype wins fading fast. With deliberate and focused efforts, what feels distant and unrealistic income wise today manifests tomorrow as new normal.

CHAPTER TWO

Getting Started

Developing an online money making mindset

Own Terms

Imagine waking up whenever your body feels rested. No blaring alarm clock. No more choosing between braving a freezing commute or dealing with your micromanaging boss' bad mood.

Instead, warm sunlight beams through window blinds. You stretch without urgency and contemplate how to spend the next few hours. Maybe crank out a new podcast episode later. Or work ahead on your latest affiliate ebook between breaks playing with the new puppy bounding around your home office.

Sound like fiction if chained to a conventional 9 to 5 job? Perhaps for now. But reshaping beliefs around how income works unlocks this lifestyle dream into reality.

Making ongoing money online first requires adopting empowering frameworks about how value transfers in modern economies. Outdated assumptions that time directly equates money earned start dissolving. And new mental rules centered on serving audience needs in scalable ways set the stage for true time and location freedom.

This chapter unpacks key principles comprising an online income mindset built to multiply earnings. Think of them as new commandments for the digital age contrasting old-school employee mindsets. They drive the behaviors and choices that consistently generate revenue no matter where you live or what you currently sell.

Embrace Abundance and Possibilities

Traditional career paths train us to view income through a lens of rigid scarcity and limitation. We must fight others for scarce promotions or client budgets. But online income flip scripts about money making as a fixed pie only allowing tiny crumbs per person.

By leveraging digital tools and global connectivity, value creation and earnings grow exponentially versus linearly. Someone consuming your digital product or affiliate recommendation now does not hinder another sale. Each person helped expands the collective pie without limit.

See past false constructs about limited taxpayer budget pots or promotions. Adopt an abundant mindset recognizing no ceiling on potential income generated or individuals served online.

Provide Ongoing Value, Not Just Transactions

Employees exchange time for dollars in defined increments. Work hour goes in, uniform wages exit out. But savvy online earners shift away from solely selling moments in time or discrete products. They deliver value on an ongoing basis.

That might mean an evergreen online course continually educating new students for years. Or building an affiliate site offering recommendations sustained through updates. The key? Structure offerings where much of the initial effort creates lasting residual value. That value gets compounded over time through reinvestments to serve more people.

So rather than fixate on immediate sales numbers each day, make choices favoring repeat engagement and access to your knowledge even when not working directly. The personal leverage is astounding.

Data and Systems Over Guesswork

Pre-internet, careers relied largely on guesswork and hopes something worked for customers. But online analytics provide concrete data, testing and insights on improving results. Track detailed metrics on content and promotion performance. Gather audience feedback. Experiment across platforms. Then build systems around approaches delivering outcomes.

Online income earners adopt growth mindset recognizing failures hold key data to tweak efforts until discovering what reliably works based on real market response. Outcomes become far less random when you embrace statistics and evidential learning.

Automate Where Possible

Rather than exclusively trade hours for dollars one batch manual labor at a time, leverage tools that multiply output. For example, email autoresponders continuously engage new subscribers without ongoing effort after setup. Automated webinars present pre-recorded info to more people simultaneously. Built once, promote forever.

Seek opportunities to create something once with upfront effort that automates value delivery over time. The compound effect on earning potential is staggering while regaining personal time freedom.

Diversify Income Streams

Most jobs coerce dependence on one single employer. But base hits add up. Combining multiple online income types hedges against disruption to any one stream. Losing an affiliate deal won't crater everything if also selling online courses and services.

Build diverse income vehicles like affiliate promotions, digital products, sponsored content, freelancing etc. Allow successes to fund testing new options while minimizing risk exposure.

Provide Extreme Value

Actually serving people's needs is table stake requirement in competitive online space. But go further by over-delivering on value beyond expectations. How can you elevate benefit for money paid? What problems can you preemptively solve? Be fanatical about the experience received from each interaction.

Online income eyed purely as dollars detached from human impact behind those dollars remains elusive. But obsess over value provided first, revenue naturally follows.

Adopt an Iterative Growth Mindset

View income production as an ever evolving process, not defined outcome. Few online efforts explode overnight without years refining strategy. But tweaking approaches based on consumer response and market testing unlocks bigger impact over time.

Patience and persistence determines long run financial results, not immediate pay days. So rather than search for perfection immediately, take progress steps trusting compound interest kicks in.

Progress Over Perfection

Tying income directly to each work hour pressures perfect output every minute. But basing money on lasting value uncouples from tallying each hour. Doing so provides freedom trying new ideas without requiring flawless output immediately. You can brainstorm blogs, test podcast concepts, tweak online course setups. Only improvements and iterations raising value matter, not each momentary result.

Online income detached from time is a game of progress aggregation. Small gains accumulate into big monetary and lifestyle payoffs over months and years.

So adapt mindsets and beliefs to support these online money principles rather than limit possibilities. Outsized income potential exists for those ignoring outdated assumptions of trading time for money. Reframe beliefs around your inherent value and online vehicles allowing that value to compound.

Then by serving people, understanding data, building systems and diversifying income streams, you manifest an abundant income lifestyle once seeming unfathomable shackled to that old employee mindset. But through proven online frameworks, bringing more value to the world synthetically attracts financial upside without perceived ceilings.

Skills & Tools Needed For Success

Here is a detailed section on the key skills and tools needed for success in making money online:

Critical Skills & Tools for Online Income Success

While anyone can technically earn income online, building consistent and sizable revenue streams long-term requires cultivating underlying competencies. Sure, rudimentary sites flung together overnight might pocket some loose affiliate change short-term through sheer luck. But without robust skills supporting your efforts, income generation eventually sputters then stalls.

To unlock lasting online profitability as skills compound, dedicate focus towards developing these fundamental areas:

Digital Marketing Skills

Marketing remains the engine driving online income efforts. So at minimum grasp essentials like search engine optimization, email outreach, social media promotion, content creation and basic funnel optimization. Being able to cost-effectively drive and convert visitors to buying customers determines profit upside.

Fortunately, endless free educational resources exist across blogs, YouTube, forums etc to build digital marketing abilities today without formal training. Prioritize a "need to know" mindset acquiring specific tactical skills for your business needs rather than overly broad theory.

Writing & Content Creation

Nearly all online monetization models rely on content matched with consumer intent to drive traffic, engagement and conversions. Short-form social posts, long-form blog content, video, podcasts, eBooks...all leverage the written word.

Develop competent writing skills across formats tailored to your audience. Outsource what you cannot effectively handle to freelancers. Recognize that over time, content output velocity, creativity and resonance with readers makes or breaks income growth.

Data & Analytics Proficiency

Online platforms provide unprecedented data on audience behavior, engagement rates, conversion performance etc. Leverage numbers to guide decisions through a ruthless focus on outcomes, not guesses. Know basic web analytics tools like Google Analytics to track key site metrics and campaign performances.

Savvy online earners adopt an experimentation mindset using data insights to determine what works rather than relying on intuition. Let statistics reveal winning patterns worth systematizing.

Audience Building Skills

Income generation relies on access to buyers. Learn methodology for cost-effectively building clearly defined audience personas over time. Nurture community cultivation across both free and paid channels like social media, content, digital advertising etc.

Monitor subscriber metrics like cost per acquisition, lifetime value and churn to optimize efforts. Without understanding audience growth tactics, online profits hit ceilings fast.

Basic Tech Literacy

Comfort traversing digital landscapes allows you to setup the technical infrastructure enabling online income. For example, tasks like hosting websites, configuring sales funnels, email delivery, webinar platforms etc.

While outsourcing complex technical work is fine, know enough to troubleshoot problems, spot incompetent vendors and ensure everything functions properly. When income depends on technology, tech literacy becomes critical.

Mindset & Self Education Ethic

Curiosity and lifelong learning willingness enables mastering the many layered competencies required to earn online over time. With so many moving parts across technology, writing, marketing, analytics and business strategy, complacency kills income potential.

Assume you will never know enough. Commit to ongoing self-education by reading books, taking courses, listening to podcasts and more on relevant online income skills. The most successful earners adopt continuous growth mindsets.

Alongside skill building, deploying tools supporting online income frameworks maximizes potential. Essential toolbox elements include:

- Website hosting
- Email list manager
- Payment processor
- Sales funnel software
- Affiliate software
- Keyword research tools
- Marketing analytics
- Sales & conversion tracking
- Basic image editor
- Office productivity software

Combined, foundational skills and supportive tools equip you to effectively monetize ideas, traffic, knowledge and products through vehicles like affiliate marketing, freelancing, coaching or information products. They give control to execute on opportunities once dependent on employers.

Of course this reflects just a starting point toolkit. Deploy more sophisticated solutions over time as income scales up. But focus first on cultivating core abilities rather than glossy tech alone. Skills unlock true earnings potential. Tools simply maximize that potential.

By dedicating consistent time habituating these fundamental skills and deploying essential tools, you construct the framework and capacity necessary to hit impressive online income goals month over month. But skipping foundational competencies often stunts income fast despite fancy funnels or spending big on ads. Simply put, skills pay the bills.

The good news? Anyone willing to put in work can develop these abilities over time for free. No prerequisite genius required. Just be strategic acquiring the building blocks enabling online income vehicles to thrive rather than randomly grasping at quick fixes and shiny objects. Channel energy into acquiring future-proof skills yielding compounding returns as expertise deepens.

Tips For Beginners - Where To Start

Eager to quit your job and start generating a full-time income online but not sure where to begin? As overwhelming as breaking into online entrepreneurship may seem initially, follow these strategic first steps to gain momentum:

Pick One Primary Income Stream

Rather than randomly trying 10 different online money tactics all at once, deeply explore one methodology first. For beginners without a following yet, affiliate marketing represents a smart starting point requiring little upfront investment. Alternatively, explore a freelancing niche or social media monetization avenue matching interests and abilities.

Deliberately specializing in one area builds foundational skills faster versus fragmented efforts. Give at least 6 months diligently honing abilities for that income type prior to diversifying. Doing too much simultaneously early on risks stagnating development in any one money vehicle.

Start Building Your Audience

Gaining access to engaged prospective buyers provides the fuel enabling all online monetization models to thrive long-term. So in parallel to perfecting say affiliate promotion tactics on a niche site, deploy content and outreach cultivating an audience aligned with topics and offers.

Audience size barely matters initially. Focus first on quality over quantity by nurturing a small group highly engaged followers. That might simply mean an email list of friends and family to start. Just take deliberate steps daily expanding reach. The compound effect over months and years is stunning regarding income potential.

Limit Upfront Costs

Rather than assume needing fancy paid tools or expensive courses to start, initially leverage free resources to build skills and test ideas. For example, start a basic affiliate review website through low-cost hosting like HostGator instead of paying for an overly complex funnel builder.

Minimize expenses until income validates investments make financial sense. Skills and sweat equity far outweigh technology or software costs when launching online income efforts.

Don't Quit Your Day Job (Yet)

Particularly for total beginners, assume online revenue needs months ramping up while dedicating nights and weekends. Very few replace full-time salaries immediately without existing platforms. Be realistic on timelines to mitigate premature risk leaving stable income sources.

The flexibility working a parallel job initially also allows freely experimenting on side projects without pressure to instantly replace essential living expenses.

Embrace Imperfection & Failures

Perfectionism kills progress. Avoid overthinking launch strategies or setups. For example, release an unpolished podcast episode, pitch that client below rates, or soft launch that online course with barebones content to start getting real market feedback fast to dictate improvements rather than hiding efforts until deemed flawless internally.

Progress made trumps endless overanalysis without action. Adjust approaches based on real customer data, testing and iterative enhancements rather than assumptions on what should work. Imperfect progress fuels evolutions toward excellence.

Adopt Ongoing Learning Lifestyle

Rapidly evolving digital landscapes demand commitment to ongoing self-education just to keep skillsets current and expanding. Dedicate consistent time each week towards reading, courses, podcasts and other resources leveling up abilities across marketing, tech tools, sales methods and more.

Mindsets resistant to constant learning cap income potential quickly. Maintain beginner's mindset forever through insatiable curiosity towards mastering evolving best practices.

Connect with Online Income Communities

Beyond formal learning resources, immense value comes from exchanging ideas with other online earners through forums, masterminds, conferences and networking groups. Find positive people tackling similar goals for collaboration, troubleshooting, accountability and inspiration tapping into their knowledge rather than exclusively figuring everything alone.

Forums like the Warrior Forum connect millions of online entrepreneurs and experts globally across nearly every conceivable digital monetization topic. Facebook Groups provide similar access to focused communities related to your niche.

Remain Patient But Persistent

Amassing marketable skills and sustainable online income relies on consistency over long time frames more than instant overnight success fantasies. Understand results often come slower than originally hoped despite diligent efforts. But trust compound progress by incrementally improving abilities, content and visibility pays significant dividends over months and years.

The biggest determiner of ultimate online income success traces back to stubborn persistence rather than pure talent. Stay patient but keep taking next steps.

Implementing these foundational tips positions online income beginners to gain traction smoothly while optimizing limited time available via focus and priority. Start simple gaining momentum in one area, connect with helpful communities, control avoidable costs and iterate based on real market feedback.

While ensuring perfect work-life balance across parallel income streams poses challenges initially, stick it out by laying sturdy foundations now that make scaling financial freedom possible within a few years rather than forever tinkering aimlessly around margins of mediocrity. Take it step-by-step. Future income potential remains bright for those starting right.

CHAPTER THREE

Affiliate Marketing

Unlocking Passive Profits Through Affiliate Marketing

Imagine waking up to notifications that someone just purchased $97 of products from your website. Then, two more sales roll in while eating breakfast. By the time lunch arrives, you tally over $500 generated that morning across a dozen orders with zero active selling efforts.

Sound like an impossible fantasy? Welcome to affiliate marketing, a monetization model allowing you to earn commissions promoting products created by other companies without ever dealing with logistics like creation, customer service or fulfillment of what's being sold. Yes – you get paid and the merchant handles everything else!

But how does one tap into this hands-off income stream exactly? And what does the process look like to start earning affiliate commissions even as early beginner with a tiny audience?

Let's explore step-by-step what affiliate marketing entails and how the paydays start flowing in...

What Is Affiliate Marketing?

Affiliate marketing represents an automated income stream based on earning an agreed upon commission every time someone purchases a product after clicking your special tracking link leading to that merchant. So for example, if you have an affiliate partnership with a SaaS company offering a $100 per month tool and convert 5 sales per month through your link, you would generate $500 per month from those referrals with no extra effort beyond the original promotion.

The company paying you handles all product fulfillment, customer service and payments collection. Yet they still share the profit with you as the affiliate since you referred the business. So you get rewarded for your marketing efforts while externalizing the heavy lifting parts of running a business to the merchant. That my friends is passive income at its finest!

Why Does Affiliate Marketing Work So Well?

For merchants, affiliate partnerships provide powerful marketing leverage tapping into niche influencers capable of precisely targeting potential customers aligned with products at scale. Rather than paying upfront for advertising, they only reward partners who generate tangible ROI on spend.

For partners like yourself, you gain instant access to high commission backend offers without needing to create any products yourself. By aligning your content and audience carefully to merchant verticals, streams of passive affiliate income start flowing in perpetually.

How Affiliate Links & Cookies Work

Rather than share generic product links, affiliates access specialized tracking URLs or ID codes containing your unique user ID embedded. For example, www.awesometool.com/?aff=JOHN243. Accessing the product through that custom link tags anyone who purchases later via a tracking cookie storing your affiliate ID on their device for 30-90 days.

So even if they don't buy instantly after clicking over from your link, the merchant still knows to credit you for driving the business if they return anytime within that cookie period and complete the transaction. This means weeks and months of potential earnings from a single visitor without repeated direct promotions. One strategic referral easily converts into recurring passive income thanks to the short term cookie continuously checking each visit.

Maximizing Affiliate Commissions

Not all affiliate programs pay equally well. The most profitable ones operate in markets with pricey products solving high priority issues for businesses and individuals. Markets like software, finance, insurance, B2B services, training courses etc. represent prime spheres. The most successful affiliates carefully cherrypick partnerships only in verticals they can authentically promote online to aligned target audiences through content on websites, emails, social media etc. Rather than spam links randomly, thoughtful niche selection and audience building around those niches amplifies conversion rates and affiliate income exponentially over time.

Additionally, prioritize partners offering exceptionally high commissions between 40-90% per sale. For digital info products, partners more commonly share 50%+ of all revenues generated. These generous payout mechanics allow capitalizing on just a handful of sales to meet income goals. Tracking down the highest paying affiliate programs with strong alignment to existing audience and niche takes a bit more due diligence upfront, but perpetually maximizes profits month over month.

While affiliate marketing may seem intimidating breaking in, know that regular people consistently generate 5 to 6 figure years without crazy tech skills or pre-existing followings across social media and websites fueling referral sales. By understanding the core concepts of providing value via content to targeted niches who actually benefit from recommendations to stellar merchant partners, unleashing passive income through affiliate marketing remains entirely accessible to anyone determined enough to put in the initial work.

But those passive paydays only materialize through deliberate effort nurturing that value-focused audience, building conversion pathways along the customer journey to merchant sites and forging partnerships with vendors incentivized to compensate you handsomely. Choose wisely and let affiliate income flow!

Top Affiliate Programs to Join

As awareness grows about the passive income potential affiliate marketing holds, curiosity follows for which specific programs offer the most lucrative opportunities currently.

Rather than sift through thousands of platforms hit-or-miss, accelerate affiliate success by selectively partnering only with verified high-value offers maximizing income.

But what constitutes a truly high-value affiliate program exactly? The sweet spot looks for vendors paying extremely generous recurring commissions while solving expensive pain points for clearly defined business or consumer niches.

Whether you're blogger, podcaster, YouTuber or social media influencer, consider exploring partnerships with these outstanding programs first when ready to tap into backend affiliate commissions:

ConvertKit - Email Marketing Software

Recommended For: Bloggers, content creators

ConvertKit makes email marketing user friendly for bloggers while offering an extremely fair affiliate program compensating partners 30% lifetime commissions. Their superior conversion technology, intuitive workflows and integrations with other creator tools like online course platforms drives consistent sales volume upon nurturing an audience. Expect average cart values ranging $50-$300+ considering implement required to scale online business.

Kajabi - Online Course Platfor

Recommended For: Bloggers, influencers, experts

Kajabi powers the backend technology for selling online courses, memberships, and other digital education products. With products averaging $100-$500 per transaction with extensive retention options, their 45% affiliate commissions payout substantially over any students lifetime. The immense value Kajabi provides solving digital education delivery makes promoting affiliate offers abundantly easy when nurturing aligned audiences seeking that knowledge.

HostGator - Web Hosting Company

Recommended For: Bloggers, developers

HostGator provides web hosting essentials allowing you to get websites online, connect domains and scale bandwidth needs over time. With baseline shared hosting plans starting around $100+ yearly paired with enormous 50% average affiliate commissions, HostGator makes an easy recurring platform to endorse even outside technical niche markets due to universal domain/hosting needs. Expect average orders ranging $100 to $500+.

SiteGround – Premium Web Hosting

Recommended For: Developers, tech influencers

SiteGround fills an easy backend affiliate opportunity niche selling premium web hosting packages running $100 to $500 yearly. Shared commissions range 60%+ for market-leading website hosting targeting buyers wanting robust solutions for high traffic, security and scalability. Value propositions sell themselves when audiences recognize SiteGround strengths. Expect bigger initial sales and stellar residual income over time.

Awin - Affiliate Network

Recommended For: Bloggers, marketers

Rather than apply individually to hundreds of affiliate programs, Awin provides access to over 13,000 merchants globally across nearly any niche imaginable – tech tools, web services, fashion, travel, finance etc. Just get approved once through their network then access and promote thousands of affiliate offers with reliable tracking, reporting and payouts all in one dashboard. Deep niche targeting options exist, although commissions vary more wildly based on each vendor.

In summary, focusing affiliate efforts around recommendations matching audience interests almost always overpowers generic sales pitches. Seek programs solving expensive problems that align with content themes and buyer needs. Customer service burdens get eliminated through automation as passive income compounds.

While the above list provides a launch point unpacking the passive profit potential waiting through affiliate, hundreds of outstanding programs exist once you identify customer pain points needing solutions. Maximizing commissions involves consistently providing extreme value on needs. Do that well and affluent affiliate income flows abundantly.

Driving targeted traffic to affiliate links

Here is a detailed overview of effective tactics for driving targeted traffic to affiliate links:

Understanding affiliate marketing concepts seems straightforward enough at surface level:

- Get approved to promote products
- Share special links
- Earn commissions when people buy

But the real art and skill behind generating a steady stream of affiliate income centers on fulfilment abilities driving targeted, high intent website traffic to those recommendation links.

Generic links haphazardly scattered across random blog posts and social media updates eventually roadblock income fast despite some initial traction. Maximizing affiliate revenue relies on crafting content and implementing promotion strategies specifically optimized to convert site visitors into buyers for the merchant products you've aligned with.

Let's unpack battle-tested traffic tactics to send legions of buyers to partner links:

Create Detailed Reviews & Demo Content

Rather than randomly insert text links within irrelevant blog posts, ensure affiliate links get embedded inside dedicated product reviews or feature demonstrations about the exact solutions potential buyers are evaluating. These expose audiences to affiliate offers within logically relevant contexts.

For example, if promoting web hosting services through SiteGround, craft comprehensive reviews spotlighting

SiteGround tools on their speeds, uptimes and technical capabilities versus alternative options. Showcase demo videos displaying the admin dashboard and site migration workflows. Outline pricing breakdowns across plan tiers helping match appropriate services with reader needs.

Such purposeful reviews and demo content add immense value helping prospects make informed decisions while seamlessly linking to affiliate offers once enough education gets established justifying your recommendation claims.

Optimize Landing Pages for Conversions

Create dedicated sales funnel landing pages laser focused on specific affiliate offers rather than just linking to external merchant sites. Guide prospects through ordering flows with relevant education for that product, incentives urging action and follow up contact options continuing relationship after purchase.

Well-designed landing pages lift conversion rates substantially compared to generic affiliate links by better controlling user experiences. Just ensure transparency on financial relationships maintained throughout.

Promote Affiliate Posts Through SEO

Expanding organic search visibility for affiliate content represents a free method driving higher volumes of targeted buyers compared to other fast fizzling paid ads channels.

But earning prominent search rankings relating to popular products takes significant upfront optimization across keyword targeting, metadata, internal linking structures, page speed, etc.

Start with buyer-oriented keywords and topic clusters pulling in commercial intent visitors more inclined to purchase solutions recommended after absorbing the educational aspects on a page. Continuously tweak On-Page elements and Off-Page signals through external references to lift standings over time. Patience pays as rankings climb.

Retarget Engaged Visitors

Even the most targeted first-touch content only converts so many users immediately.

Retargeting ads keep your affiliate offers in front of engaged visitors through platforms like Google, Facebook and native advertising networks after leaving initial website touchpoints via pixels installed.

Lookalike profiling also helps discover more users resembling the target demographic attributes and interests of pastconverted affiliate buyers.

Consider also adding email follow up sequences capturing site visitor contact info through lead magnet incentives in exchange for downloadables like product cheat sheets, comparison charts etc.

Effective affiliate marketers view every impression as progress moving potential customers closer to eventual conversion.

Follow up strategies connect the breadcrumbs for visitors to complete the journey over time.

Transition Content into Video, Audio & Community

Expand mediums beyond the blog over time. Podcast interviews add personality and commentary value versus purely clinical product analysis rundowns. YouTube review videos showcase aesthetics in action for tangible demos. And forum discussions provide access to real user experiences determining how offers truly stack up.

Varying content formats and community sourcing helps buyers connect with options recommended on deeper levels as they evaluate next steps.

Affiliates purely chasing payment notifications without understanding core traffic fundamentals strangle their upside fast. But by crafting high value educational resources finely tuned to merchant offers you believe in across multiple platforms, targeted buyers continue discovering your recommendations organically for months and years.

Seed that automated passive income through patience crafting positioned content driving steady conversion streams over time. Consistent value fuels impact and affiliate rewards.

Most Common Affiliate Marketing Mistakes to Avoid

Here is an in-depth overview of the most common affiliate marketing mistakes to avoid:

With the freedom and profit potential of affiliate marketing so compelling, beginners eagerly jump in hoping quick passive paydays follow shortly behind minimal effort.

But without understanding core strategic principles guiding sustainable affiliate success, subpar results usually reflect reality until eventually channeling energy elsewhere.

Before abandoning affiliate income potential though, audit approach against these common pitfalls sabotaging earning upside early on:

Taking a Generalized Approach

Successful affiliates carefully niche down website content and promotions catering to tightly focused buyer personas rather than covering broad universal interest topics.

For example, an outdoor recreation site might segment camping gear recommendations from hiking, mountain biking, overlanding vehicle setups etc. This allows targeting affiliate offers around the micro needs of each distinct audience rather than assuming 1-size-fits-all content applies to any subsection evenly.

Get incredibly specific identifying core needs and problems for a well defined audience to precision target affiliate solutions matching their interests.

Neglecting Relationship Building

Random strangers rarely click oddly positioned affiliate links without context or clearly defined value propositions stated upfront. Yet, far too many affiliates prioritize payments over audience connection absent trust and familiarity. They blast out thin blog posts littered with affiliate links hoping breezy passive profits follow despite little community nurturing.

Flip mindsets away from faceless users to forging genuine relationships around needs a carefully chosen affiliate offer can satisfy long-term. Rather than chase short-term transactions, dedicate upfront efforts understanding audience challenges and building authority positioning you as subject matter experts around those topics over time. Introduce affiliate links only once earned audience trust and clarity surfaces on how your recommendation specifically powers their success.

Lacking Quality Content

Google and savvy internet users easily recognize thin content published primarily for earning affiliate commissions rather than solving information needs. But despite warnings, low quality blog posts existing solely to funnel users blindly towards affiliate links persist across the web.

Understand that search engines and readers prioritize solutions publishing extensive, in-depth and often unique insider knowledge on topics before casually suggesting any related products in periphery. Detailed content earns attention and amplifies conversions. Sparse content urges bounce backs.

Prioritizing Peak Earning Products

Chasing maximum headline commission rates often backfires for affiliates eventually. Vetting product viability matters more than purely big payout percentages.

Rather than promoting on pricey upsells with questionable true market demand solely for higher backend payout checks, ensure affiliate products recommended undeniably enhance audience lives first with pricing reasonably affordable to segmented users. Mismatched products and audiences pay little long-run.

Abandoning Too Early

Many affiliates barely wait few months before declaring the income model fundamentally flawed after minimal earnings gathered. But slow initial momentum while honing abilities proves entirely normal before witnessing growth at scale.

Temper expectations around reasonable timelines understanding affiliate sites earn little initially while dedicating Phase 1 establishing foundational pillars like content and audience. But over subsequent years, assets compound allowing far easier replication of what works for exponentially growing income.

Give efforts sufficient runway through an investment mindset before determining efficacy. Consider initial slow earnings as tuition while skill building rather than instant jackpots.

Not Tracking Performance

Substantial affiliate opportunities exist to promote products genuinely helping audiences progress. But without monitoring analytics gauging content resonation and campaign success identifying what converts best, guesses replace fact-based data separating top earning affiliates over time.

Obsess over metrics highlighting engagement rates, conversions, commission sizes etc rather than passively awaiting payments. Refine repeatedly around what moves numbers most over time.

If underperforming so far affiliate marketing-wise, conduct inventory against these common stumbling blocks before abandoning income potential. Refocus efforts on quality over quantity across authority building, niche audience connection and providing extreme value on interests. That strong base compounds over time eclipsing early setbacks. But failure to course correct continues flatlining income indefinitely unless confronting core strategic adjustments separating success stories from cautionary tales.

With the right foundational pillars erected early on, affiliate passivity reality starts matching the hype across Guides like this aimed at steering newbies towards prosperity over financial false starts.

CHAPTER FOUR

Popular Online Freelancing Platforms

Here are some of the most popular online freelancing platforms:

1. Upwork - One of the largest freelance websites with millions of clients posting jobs from over 180 countries. Upwork has jobs in many categories like web development, design, writing, administration and more.

2. Fiverr - Fiverr is a top marketplace for freelance services focused on gigs with starting prices at $5. It's ideal for freelancers offering specific services like graphic

design, writing, video editing, programming.

3. Freelancer - A global platform with over 5 million employers and freelancers registered. Jobs span hundreds of categories from data entry to software development to finance.

4. Toptal - A more premium network connecting elite freelancers with top companies. Very selective on talent but work pays well and steady for accepted freelancers. Focus is on software development, design and finance.

5. Guru - Guru has over 3 million freelancers and 1.5 million employers collaborating largely in IT, admin and

creative project work. Known for openness to hiring globally distributed talent.

6. PeoplePerHour - PeoplePerHour connects SMEs with freelancers for project work across IT, marketing, admin and more. 2.4 million registered freelancers and counting.

7. FlexJobs - FlexJobs specializes in connecting professional freelancers to jobs from thousands of prescreened, legitimate companies. Paid subscriptions but very reputable curated leads.

8. SolidGigs - Solidgigs publishes handpicked, verified, high-quality freelance job leads across categories like writing, editing, social media marketing etc. for members getting alerts.

I'd recommend new freelancers explore a few general marketplaces first like Upwork and Fiverr to establish reviews and experience handling different client projects. From there, consider specializing on one or two premium networks closely aligned with specific skill niches further into the freelance journey.

Developing a Compelling Freelancer Profile

Crafting a compelling freelancer profile is crucial for attracting clients and standing out in crowded marketplaces like Upwork, Fiverr or Freelancer. Here are tips for developing an effective profile:

1. Include a professional profile photo to build trust and approachability. Dress professionally and smile.

2. Write a detailed yet scannable headline and overview section summarizing your services, experience and skills. Use relevant keywords clients search.

3. Showcase specific examples of previous work through a portfolio highlighting successes and client outcomes achieved.

4. Feature client reviews and testimonials to build credibility leveraging social proof.

5. Clearly communicate your expertise in written content and skills tags by outlining distinct service offerings, industries served, and types of projects completed already.

6. Emphasize availabilities and responsiveness conveying reliability delivering on time.

7. List all relevant certifications, awards, press features or education establishing authority.

8. Convey personality and approachability through your writing tone, images and video introductions.

9. Specify preferred project types, budgets and client expectations to attract ideal matching opportunities.

10. Stand out by expanding beyond basic text-based profiles through video introductions explaining services.

Compelling freelancer profiles capture attention quickly through professional presentation and top-notch content while also building trust and approachability humanizing your abilities to incentivize contact. Put your best foot forward and get noticed for the right freelance gigs.

Top Freelancing Gigs For Beginners

Here is an overview of top freelancing gigs suitable for beginners to get started:

1. Virtual Assistant Services

With some basic admin skills and communication abilities, virtual assistants help clients with tasks like email management, scheduling, data entry and research projects. It's an accessible intro gig teaching responsiveness working directly supporting teams.

2. Blog Writing

Beginner freelance writers can build portfolio samples and earn solid rates writing blogs for companies on trending topics and news related to business, technology and various industries.

3. Graphic Design

Tools like Canva make basic graphic design approachable for non-designers. Beginners can offer services creating social media posts, ads, flyers, posters, infographics, and presentations on a contract basis for clients.

4. Data Entry

Attention to detail matters most beginning with data entry gigs inputting and organizing information for businesses and research firms through platforms like Amazon Mechanical Turk. Build accuracy and speed.

5. Customer Service

Newbie freelancers adept at communicating can offer customer service assistance handling inquiries, moderating online communities and delivering frontline support as virtual call center reps.

6. Transcription Services

Convert audio and video files to text documents transcribing meetings, interviews, speeches and more. Typically a fixed rate per audio hour as you gain precision and typing speeds.

7. Translation Services

Bilingual freelancers can provide translation services tackling projects converting documents and media from one language to another. Nail quality first before boosting project volumes.

8. Video Editing

Basic video editing like clipping footage, inserting transitions, adding text/graphics and exporting cleaned up finished productions gets outsourced regularly on beginner rates.

The benefit testing different introductory gigs allows sampling multiple freelance verticals to determine best niche fits long-term based on competencies and interests. Land first clients focusing locally initially through community boards and personal networks to build reputations and reviews transitioning eventually into higher paying international contracts.

Tips For Successfully Winning First Clients

Landing those critical first clients when starting a business can seem like a monumental hurdle. However, with some strategic preparation and outreach, you can position yourself for success in acquiring inaugural customers. First, ensure you have honed your offerings and know who you want to serve. Outline your services, identify your ideal client profile, and craft customized pitches.

An essential step is networking – both online and locally. Attend trade events, conferences, or seminars to connect face-to-face with potential clients. Come prepared with business cards and a polished elevator pitch that summarizes what problem you solve. Follow up promptly with new contacts after events to further conversations. Similarly, actively engage on social media channels popular with your targets. Provide value by commenting insightfully, answering questions, and joining related groups. The connections and credibility built can yield leads.

Leveraging existing contacts can also give a credibility boost for securing those first sales. Consider reaching out to past colleagues, bosses, mentors, or even your personal network. Let them know you started this business and would appreciate referrals or introductions. People are often happy to help, especially if you aided them previously during your relationship.

When you have identified promising leads, tailor outreach to resonate with their needs. Personalize emails or cold calls to showcase you grasp their challenges. Offer a free consultation, highlight relevant case studies, and convey why you're uniquely positioned to deliver results. Be persistent yet gracious with follow-ups but also know when to walk away and refocus efforts elsewhere.

Now for the actual sales conversion process, instill confidence by thoroughly answering questions and addressing concerns. Convey your passion for the field and highlight specialized skills or credentials. Provide concrete examples of outcomes you've enabled for similar customers. If appropriate, offer special incentives like discounts or expanded services to secure a first deal.

Landing page and website copy also matter, so ensure messaging aligns with client priorities. Emphasize skill sets, expertise levels and how you can propel their business goals. Include strong calls to action to contact you for initial discussions.

Leverage client testimonials or case studies if available even from past roles to reinforce credibility. However, if launching completely new offers, consider pilot projects with key contacts to obtain proof points for marketing.

Stay vigilant even after winning some early business by requesting introductions to colleagues needing your services or asking to provide additional services. Keep focusing on delivering exceptional value, results, and relationship-building to cement loyalty for ongoing and expanded business.

Remember that tenacity, personal outreach, persuasiveness, and commanding industry expertise are instrumental. Remain patient through what could be a challenging but ultimately rewarding process to convert those first monumental clients. Then continue optimizing your sales strategies to grow. With the right preparation and persistence, you will be primed for acquiring trailblazing customers to set your business' trajectory upward.

CHAPTER FIVE

Creating Passive Income Through Information Products

Types of profitable informational products

In the digital age, informational products present tremendous business opportunities. By packaging your knowledge and expertise into online assets delivered instantly, you can generate income through multiple streams. From established authorities to enterprising entrepreneurs, anyone can leverage their wisdom to create lucrative informational products.

eBooks

One of the most common and accessible formats is the eBook - essentially book-form content produced as digital files. eBooks allow creating long-form, text-based assets spanning 50-250 pages that buyers can download as PDFs, EPUBs, or other readable files. They can tackle elaborate concepts, technical processes, or tactical advice unpacked through chapters and sections. You can produce eBooks on almost any topic from DIY guides to business methods to niche industry lessons. Integrate text, images, charts, or other multimedia for an engaging reader experience. eBooks can earn profits by selling copies or charging subscription fees for updated versions.

Courses

Online courses allow structuring lessons and training content into organized learning pathways. Like an eBook, you can tackle broad topics but deliver the informational through video tutorials, slide decks, quiz assessments, and more. Students can progress through self-paced or cohort-based courses with community discussion forums. Courses can be sold individually or within memberships whilebranded course platforms can be marketed as premium offerings. They can be excellent income generators especially for highly specialized knowledge.

Templates & Tools

Leveraging your expertise to produce templates, planners, calculators, trackers, and other tools to simplify complex tasks or guide buyers can also prove profitable. Help audiences organize information through smart spreadsheets, printable guides, slide decks, and more. Offer a library of customizable documents and digital assets applied to various business or life functions. While individuals may purchase pieces ala carte, template bundles and memberships provide ongoing value through updated collections.

Podcasts

Both audio and video podcasts present opportunities to generate revenue from informational content. Release free episodes covering targeted topics to attract a loyal following. Once you build an engaged audience, leverage avenues like sponsorships, ad placements, affiliate marketing, listener support memberships and more for monetization. Dedicated fans will pay for extras like transcripts, guides, discussion communities and additional content.

Newsletters

Email newsletters continue offering profit making potential by allowing you to reach invested subscribers seeking insights. Offer free newsletters covering topics they care about, then implement paid upgrades for premium editions, access member-content or crowdsource support to fund expanded offerings. Integrate affiliate links or advertising to further newsletter monetization.

Consulting & Coaching

Package your niche mastery into personalized consulting, advising, skill development and coaching across fields like business, health, and technology. Sell blocks of one-on-one time for tailor-made guidance to meet individual client challenges. Structure sessions by specialty areas with defined outcomes. Or develop exclusivity through retainer and mastermind communities. Publish strong credential markers like client outcomes to attract buyers.

The possibilities are endless for creating informational products that prioritize relevance, problem-solving and meaningful value for audiences while generating generous revenue. Determine what high-demand insights you can distill into user-friendly formats, then implement diversified distribution and pricing plans. Tap into the remarkable power that comes from profits and purpose.

Ideas and Niches For Info Products

Here are some promising ideas and niches to consider for creating informational products:

Health and Wellness

- Nutrition plans/healthy recipes
- Fitness programs
- Yoga and meditation guides
- Stress management techniques
- Natural healing alternatives
- Healthy aging and longevity

Business and Entrepreneurship

- Startup guides and planning tools
- Marketing, sales, and PR training courses
- Leadership and management ebooks
- Productivity methods and tools
- Personal finance budgeting templates
- Freelancing and side hustle ideas

Technology and Software

- Coding tutorials
- Graphic design guides
- Cybersecurity courses
- Software development ebooks
- Data analytics model templates

Personal Growth and Lifestyle

- Finding your life purpose/passion
- Organization habits and tools
- Relationship and life advice guides
- Parenting/family bonding tips
- Focus and habits model
- Travel hacking courses
- Crafts, Hobbies and DIY
- Home improvement projects
- Woodworking schematics
- Knitting and sewing patterns

- Painting techniques training
- Gardening and landscaping plans
- Auto maintenance tutorials

The key is determining subjects you have deep expertise, credibility or personal experience around that map to audiences passionate about those areas. Ideate solutions for struggles they face or results they want then design informational products catering to those needs.

Creating Your First Ebook, Video Course, Podcast, Etc.

Launching a breakout informational product may seem daunting but strategic planning and simplicity can pave the way for success. Start by identifying topics matching your capabilities with audience needs. List subjects you possess deep insights, stories or how-to knowledge regarding then find eager niches seeking that content.

Now determine what format best aligns with sharing your wisdom. eBooks, for example, work well for mixing text, images and templates to create valuable resources people can reference repeatedly. Courses allow teaching comprehensive concepts through lessons. Podcasts episodically engage listeners through intimacy, personality and nuanced storytelling.

Decide on core themes, chapter breakdowns or episode arcs before generating content. Outline takeaways readers/viewers/listeners should grasp after consuming each piece. Envision transformational before/after states they could achieve via your guidance. What concrete knowledge or steps might get them there?

Maintain focus by working in short sessions, consistently writing, recording and reviewing progress to catch lulls in energy or quality. Set daily content creation goals oriented around completing one full chapter, lesson or episode at a time. Maintain momentum working chapter-by-chapter or episode-by-episode until a full draft is done.

Now refine the structure and flow. For written products, strengthen transitions so concepts build logically. Podcasts should hook listeners quickly while ending episodes on cliffhangers teasing the next show. Weave personal anecdotes throughout all formats to forge connections through storytelling. Headline or emphasize key takeaways so they stand out clearly.

Pay special attention to openings and closings to capture attention and compulsion to continue consuming content. Wrap written products with concise "next step" guidance focused on activating reader progress. Courses should assess progress through intermittent quizzes reinforcing retention. Episode recaps and teases generate binge appeal.

With initial drafts complete,editing is critical for polished products worth purchasing. Scrutinize content addressing three key areas:

Does this provide real value? Be brutally honest assessing whether your informational product uniquely educates, entertains or transforms reader/viewers/listeners. Every component should constructively impact them.

Is it easily consumable? Reviews written pieces for dense paragraphs needing breaks into quick-hit takeaways and bullet points. Check lengthy podcast monologues or static PowerPoints that could benefit from greater dynamism through images, anecdotes and levity.

What's missing? Identify potential knowledge gaps or sections needing elaboration then create supplementary content addressing them. Ask beta consumers for feedback identifying disconnects needing bridged or landmines to avoid regarding controversial topics.

Refine, rewrite and rework pieces needing improvement. Record new dialogues or slide additions around holes found through edits and feedback. With each successive pass, you'll hone clarity, value and appeal.

Finally, assemble all organized information into a cohesive product. Compile written documents into aesthetically designed ebooks easy to navigate with clickable tables of contents and sections. Podcasts get uploaded into channels and hosting platforms. Courses may integrate with online portals facilitating lesson access, quizzes and discussions.

While launching an informational product involves effort, maintain inspiration around why you're sharing this hard-won knowledge. Envision who you can empower and problems that will be solved. Let that purpose feed your tenacity to push past hurdles. Before long you'll have crafted a resonant resource poised to educate eager audiences. Then continue building on early wins to grow your authority and profits over time.

Promoting and Selling Your Informational Product

Creating a valuable informational product is an achievement but next comes the critical work of effectively promoting it to drive sales. First, optimize external and internal marketing assets to align with core buyer priorities and irresistibly convey your expertise.

Update websites and landing pages with magnetic copy emphasizing customer struggles and tangible transformations from using your product. Weave in social proof through reviews and testimonials. Capture visitors with free previews of content then lead them through flows incentivizing purchase.

Ensure clarity on pricing and formats sold. Promote through channels popular with your niche from email lists to social media platforms to affiliate partners. Run small test campaigns to see what messaging and media most effectively converts. Offer limited-time discounts or product bundles to catalyze initial purchases during launches.

Incorporate upsells during checkout such as companion workbooks, consulting hours or exclusive member-access to future products. Savings on these items incentivize bigger immediate spend while guaranteeing future recurring revenue enabling business growth.

Post-purchase follow up is equally essential so new buyers gain full value from products, leaving them satisfied and hungry for more. Deliver smooth access and usability experience so customers easily obtain purchased digital items. Provide supplemental setup guidance or usage tips through emails or exclusive portals.

Offer exemplary customer support in case questions or problems emerge. Your responsiveness and resolve leaves lasting impressions that drive repeat purchases and referrals. Consider nurturing sequences with helpful content driving them deeper into your ecosystem.

While this post-sales experience solidifies sprang satisfaction, your work bolstering awareness never ends. Consistently showcase content samples through websites, social channels and outreach campaigns. Position yourself as the guide who solved struggles they face.

Speaking opportunities, guest interviews and contributed articles are tremendous for expanding reach. Set Google alerts to find relevant discussions to add your perspective to. Pitch yourself as a source to reporters and producers.

Leverage affiliates and partners to tap into their audiences. Negotiate promotions like discounted pricing, bundled offers or exclusive previews for their followers. Collaborate on free content highlighting each other's complementary strengths. Go on podcast tours or co-create workshops.

Study competitors and emulate their wins while avoiding missteps and forging your unique space. Outdo others' quality, features or added value. Identify rising informational products to collaborate with rather than compete against.

Keep releasing updated editions or new products to reward loyal followers with fresh, elite material not found anywhere else. Launch memberships granting VIP access and community support.

Rally early adopters as brand advocates to organically spread your content to untapped networks through reviews, social shares and casual referrals. Equip them with any affiliate resources to easily promote your offerings.

The combined impact of robust marketing mechanisms, optimizing customers' post-purchase lifecycle, maintaining industry visibility, leveraging partnerships and continually cultivating influencer relationships will compound, cementing your business as a go-to informational authority. Stay nimble adapting strategies then watch your wisdom transform lives while income grows.

CONCLUSION

The digital landscape provides immense potential for enterprising creators to package their expertise into lucrative informational products. Tap into booming niches seeking trustworthy guidance around challenges they face personally and professionally. Position yourself as the sage to lead them from confusion to clarity.

Analyze your capabilities and credentials to identify subjects you can credibly instruct audiences on through convenient online education products. Blueprint these into eBooks, video courses, templates, podcasts and more. Outline specific frustrations you help resolve along with tangible outcomes delivered through adopting your lessons.

Strategically craft content that engages and empowers, walking learners through step-by-step journeys to master lucrative skills or optimize intricate areas of life and work. Blend personalized storytelling with research and hard data so products resonate rationally and emotionally. Structure flows facilitating retention and activation with summaries, worksheets and assessments reinforcing key takeaways.

Polish products exuding quality and care through meticulous editing and revision until they deliver irresistible value far beyond pricing. Clean up structures, strengthen transitions and ensure consistency across messaging and brands. Pursue feedback to safeguard against gaps in knowledge or solutions that could undermine experiences.

Market creatively across a spectrum of channels, emphasizing conversions and customer lifecycle. Funnel website visitors through alluring free previews down sales funnel journeys. Run promotions spotlighting products as must-have solutions for niche struggles. Upsell additional items increasing transaction value. Post-purchase, overdeliver on onboarding, support and community.

Creatively amplify reach and exposure through PR pitches, guest interviews, contributor bylines, podcast tours, affiliates and collaborations. Have products discoverable and accessible exactly when audience needs arise. Become the informational authority patrons and journalists recommend when related topics emerge.

Stay perpetually relevant through updated editions, new product releases and irresistible membership sites granting VIP access. Foster loyalists and influencers to organically broadcast your brand across their trusted networks.

Soon these orchestrated strategies coalesce, connecting you with eager learners ready to purchase life-improving education. Products sell themselves as audiences realize their promise speeding progress on passions, projects and professional advancement. Each new raving fan and course graduate becomes a testament to your meaningful impact.

While informational product development and marketing contain challenges, lean into wins small and large. Let minor milestones like an initial purchase or positive feedback fuel motivation during difficult times. Maintain sight of the vision where your wisdom guides thousands to live brighter.

Trust that ambitious dreams manifest through a compounding aggregation of disciplined action, resilience towards outcomes and unrelenting belief. Soon results crescendo into profit and purpose fulfilling destinies.

So consecrate yourself to crafting resonating resources and serving communities craving your unique guidance. The rest flows naturally.

www.ingramcontent.com/pod-product-compliance
Lightning Source LLC
Chambersburg PA
CBHW070035300526
45794CB00001B/500